It Will Return

It Will Return

poems

Julia Hartwig

Translated from the Polish by John and Bogdana Carpenter

NORTHWESTERN UNIVERSITY PRESS

EVANSTON, ILLINOIS

Northwestern University Press
www.nupress.northwestern.edu

This book has been funded by the Book Institute © POLAND
Translation Program.

Printed in the United States of America

10 9 8 7 6 5 4 3 2 1

Library of Congress Cataloging-in-Publication Data
Hartwig, Julia.
    [To wróci. English]
    It will return : poems / Julia Hartwig ; translated from the Polish by John and
Bogdana Carpenter.
       p. cm.
    Includes bibliographical references.
    ISBN 978-0-8101-2678-7 (pbk. : alk. paper)
    I. Carpenter, John, 1936– II. Carpenter, Bogdana. III. Title.
    PG7167.A75T6 2010
    891.8517—dc22

                                    2009044384

CONTENTS

It Will Return

A Promise

A beautiful face
How beautiful when it returns unexpected
in a portrait from Faiyûm

A face close to us
yet sculpted by distant ages

promised forever
yet not saved

Beautiful when meditating
beautiful when sleeping
a face speechless and impenetrable

Blues

Just before
Read that parable
O yes
Read it

And don't forget to return there where
O yes
don't forget to return there

Try to understand what at that time
O yes
try to understand

And don't neglect to destroy that
you know
O yes
don't neglect

And listen to this quartet
as when
O yes
listen

because it comes so unexpectedly
it comes
O yes
so unexpectedly

Keats's Grave

The melancholy of young Keats
hovers above his grave
on a Roman hill
like a hazy sunny mist

You will abandon it to look—after Iwaszkiewicz—
at the grave of a Russian nanny
buried here by grateful émigré children

Iwaszkiewicz!
He didn't hesitate to admit
he liked to visit old cemeteries

Greatness has no scruples
to ponder on what's rotten in us
it doesn't conceal its hatreds and friendships

Respect! The motto of Goethe was taken up by Miłosz
He knew how to value in others what he lacked
But if he had it would he be himself

Daimonion

He summoned it obstinately
watching it day and night
because he knew
it is always about to flee

When he was old
he obtained in return its faithfulness
and absolute devotion

it lay down by his bed
and left together with him

To Die to Sleep

After he left did he still return to that place
where he abandoned the instrument
and taking it in his hands
did he call on the deserted world
for the trees birds and animals to return
and follow him and his pain

Or else was there "a fragrant scent of herbs, the low humming of bees,
And he fell asleep with his cheek pressed to the warm earth"

Or was he like Dante when singing the third canto
of the *Inferno:*
"a man whom sleep has seized, I fell"

Greatness

How this Norwid hurts
so proud
yet agreeing to be let in through the kitchen door

they acknowledge him from kindness
yet don't respect or care about him

It is true what they say about you:
you are great
even
among the titans

yet you always dine at the end of the table
a genial parishioner

You are proof that writing is a great sin
a deviation
not to find the place one deserves
as if it were an obligation
always to have a tie and handkerchief
a sunny room with a carefully selected view
and a meal brought in by a servant
if not by a friendly hand

Volumes of poems letters left by you
and these last words in a Parisian poorhouse:
Cover me better

Vincent

If madness in art has such power
that it paralyzes the one who looks at the painting
protect madness
and allow us to shout that we are not mad
but full of divine envy which is rapture

Why have you made him pay
for setting fire
to the wheat fields and meadows around Arles
with a rapacious sun
and for extinguishing it at sunset

A Tiger at Home

When the Douanier Rousseau
painted a tiger baring its teeth
in a jungle looking like the Jardin des Plantes
he was so frightened by the sight
he shivered and ran to the window
calling for help

If only when writing a poem or painting a picture
we could believe in it so truly
as if we created life itself

On the Theme of the Diabelli Variations

Un poco più vivace
Un poco più allegro
pesante e resoluto

The mouth seems to sing
the body floats on a wave
lips tighten

As if you were peeking at love
Un poco più mosso
Grave e maestoso

The hand sails away
Presto scherzando
A smile and sempre cantabile
adagio ma non troppo

O give us back andante
This presto is like an insult
Fughetta

The thirty-first variation
is now singing like a river a forest
Largo molto espressivo

And like a slap in the face
applause

A Choice

To throw oneself head down
from the height of the poem
to achieve the only safe
mortal equilibrium

Come Back Rimbaud

To flee Europe and throw away poetry
like an empty bag with diamonds
to forget he lived somewhere
to get rid of Verlaine
to empty his genius into forgetfulness

Come back Rimbaud
now you know what awaits you over there
you will be Someone Else

You will impersonate the merchant from Havana who requests
Damonet's *Masonry* from France
Berfthaut's *The Perfect Welder*
The Gunsmith's Guide

You will trade in arms cotton and beads
you will carry pounds of gold sewn into your belt
and withhold the donkey drivers' pay

To endure to survive You will think of that only
when suffering like a damned man
you will be carried on a stretcher
with a gangrened leg

From the hospital in Marseille
you will write your sister you would like to marry and have a family

and then: "Our life is misery
misery with no end!"

The Heart of Day

The heart of day the sun beating in us and beyond
Let all that lives be truly alive
In its even beat there is freedom and independence
in its risings and settings a natural order
against which we don't rebel

O the great joy of feeling sadness and suffering
The experience that circulates in our veins
What to do with you? What to do?

Tell Me Rabbi

When the young man heard
he had to give away all his possessions
to be saved
he became sad and left

Was he sad
because his possessions
were dearer to him than the distant prize
and the promise of immortality

The story tells only
that he was sad and left
nowhere does it say
whether he could enjoy
his possessions as before

To give away everything
Isn't it what the Word expects from us
And when it doesn't receive everything
it is sad and leaves

Sweet Armenia in Three Dimensions

An elderly couple of a dusklike age
Armenians
on a retirement trip
met at an empty café terrace on the Aegean Sea

They sit at my table to receive kindness
and to bestow kindness

How in this gentle sea air
can one keep on the surface
this dry rock of their story
again and again rolled up and out of memory

Our story and national saga
is the massacre—they say
Such is the story of our families

It happened
that we traveled across their native country
a kingdom of pastures
on broad shoulders of hills
Countless herds of grazing sheep
under the eye of a shepherd
with an Evangelical staff

We were aiming beyond the horizon
toward the holy mountain of Ararat
where Noah's Ark became stuck

One by one Turks and Armenians
were leaving it for firm land
their faces radiant

Zone

The breathing of the universe was heavy
If anything was still following the demands of art
it was a dream
but it went astray as well

Cold steps of a trek
less and less comprehensible

We all desired to be liberated
from the imposed shackles
and paragraphs were ready
but no relief

The remnants of old words were exhausted
Ashamed and humiliated
we looked for something

From Where This Consent

We really don't think about it
but on the way as if casually
we listen

Dying is hard labor
He knows what he is speaking about
because he saw
the wounded dying after a battle
hospital stretchers taking them to the morgue

We are waiting for a different story
We want to know how it is
and where this consent in us comes from
consent for separation

Breathing above their bodies the earth rises at night
the moon looks straight into their eyes
They repeat:
Yet One was resurrected

Reflections

Leaving the place behind
And always on and on
suppressing the thought there is a limit
beyond which we don't want to go

A suicidal feeling of guilt
which like original sin
is beyond repair

To bring the dead back to life
to bring back days that have passed
all this is not in our power
How to evaluate
the futility of this life

At Night in Bellagio

She stood at the window in darkness and looked
A black lake moonless sky
dark outline of stark mountains barely visible
all immersed in the secret tension of endurance

The distance from her own life was so great
the estrangement so soothing
as if souls could forget what they lived through
What did he dream about at this moment
sleeping behind her back

This Moment
when all grows calm
and such overwhelming light shines
from behind everything
from where you are

Dear ones
you who are invisible
it wasn't worth it to die

The Haunted City

New York in a storm of electric lights
Falling stars of planes landing

Pray for us holy Statue of Liberty
with glowing rays above your head

The angels' overcast foreheads flare up
the taut arc of the illuminated Verrazano Bridge
a necklace clasped on the indigo sky

Stone thresholds of New York tenements
where lovers from film melodramas
parted at night

and the deadliness of Park Avenue
its disdainful order and emptiness

Vertiginously high skyscrapers
silent about Lechoń's leap
into the abyss of Manhattan

Singing sirens of ships sailing the East River and the Bay
Your homeland is far away
and you will never go back

Thus worship the holy Statue of Liberty
and pray to it the litany of a mantra

Be blessed
Lady of our pilgrimage
Lady of winds and icy hospitality
Lady infinitely indifferent
and full of grace
Cold mother
to whom we abandoned ourselves

Neon

A hot night in a big city
Dust sweat and blood
A half-naked woman with a whip
against a sky covered with American stars
Down below the dark plebeian song
of a lost stranger

A Long Life

The oldest citizen of the United States
died at the age of 137
He was a slave brought to the States in 1854

Charlie Smith was never sure of the year of his birth
He was noticed during a citrus harvest in central Florida
He was 112
The clerks confirmed his age
after discovering documents in New Orleans
it was also confirmed by papers
found in Texas

In the last weeks before his death
Charlie slept without a break
He didn't recognize his seventy-year-old son
who came to see him
He was a sort of rarity
Shown in public
he wore a white suit over his thin body
and a black bow tie at the neck
He remembered events on the coast of his native Liberia
—Since I left
said the old man
I never saw my mother

When he was twelve he was shipped to New Orleans
where he was sold to a ranch owner in Texas
whose name was Charlie Smith
His owner bestowed on him his own name and surname
His real name was Mitchell Watkins

The slave outlived his owner
He played the banjo sang
and didn't know the meaning of worry
said the owner—my neighbor in a train compartment
going from Los Angeles to San Francisco
—Fate is unjust
Do you know how much trouble I had with my ranch?

Janis

If you already enjoy some fame
and desire above all to be adored by the crowd
die young
you will become Fortune's darling

Janis Joplin
her hoarse singing awakening the enthusiasm of millions
A hopeless cry for help
of a celebrity of the concert hall

I regret that I gave birth to you—her mother said
when Janis tried to return to Kansas
causing a sensation in the streets of her native city

I remember Joplin's voice coming one morning
from a room next to our flat on Long Island
and a refrain sung in the hoarse low voice
"Buy me a color TV"

It wasn't a recording
Unbelievably faithful to the intonation and sound
it was my daughter
imitating her voice

Cutty Sark

In the London docks fire consumed
a large part of the famous schooner *Cutty Sark*
that for more than a hundred years
transported tea from China to England

The *Cutty Sark* will be rebuilt
It faithfully served an English tradition
Tea follows the Englishman and waits for him
wherever he finds himself
cups steamed at stopping places of English units
fighting in the Second World War
volunteers served tea in London shelters
in breaks between raids

The taut sails of the *Cutty Sark*
reappear on the sea meadows
and wooden cases carefully packed
will land once again on dockers' carts

The song played by the *Cutty Sark* on waves and in the wind
is an old song in honor of tea
sung by Keats Purcell and Britten
sung in a hoarse voice by a street girl
At teatime the quarrel between Conservatives and Labour
grows silent

Laughter in the Dark

When he asked the key question
several hands went up
I too raised my hand

It seemed as if he knew me
and counted on my answer

When my turn came I suddenly understood
it was me who was entrusted
to reveal the most important thing

The panic I felt at that moment was so great
I started up out of sleep hitting my head against the wall

Delivered from the nightmare
I burst out laughing
in the dark

Where Do They Wander

We came running and he was there
amidst a crowd of pilgrims exiles fugitives

We brought him a gift in an old crumpled newspaper
He took it without looking Absentminded he glanced at us
stripped of everything mute feverish

Where was he going? He didn't know
nor did we

But we knew this is how it must be
that he has to go

We too were like abandoned parcels
without a home and without hope

Many people in the crowd were contaminated
aware that soon they will be no longer

A wonderful lady who mysteriously found herself here
sat on a high pile of dirt
with a black and white scarf over her face

We lifted the sacks of a malicious and grouchy old woman
and carried them to the next stop
We are completely alone now—I said

And it wasn't sadness but like the howling of the wind
that tugs and gnaws without reason
because this is its nature

It was not clear if we would go further
or stay here to the end
but something unknown was still flickering in us
and we abandoned ourselves to fate
not even knowing what it really means

The Unattainable

When Zimerman asked Lutosławski
how he should play one of his compositions
the composer answered:
Play casually

Only a master can speak like that
to another master
because his "casually" is a result of perfection
a ripe fruit freely falling from a tree
to ground that from the beginning had an intention to bear fruit

He once said:
The piano has no secrets for me

Trusting

When they are about ready
to enter the dangerous terrain of poetry
they choose protectors in the highest circle
trusting that in their shadow
it will be easier to conceal the clumsiness of their first steps

But with their backs to us
Pascal Nietzsche Schopenhauer and Spinoza
didn't even know they were chosen
absorbed by the thought of uncompleted tasks

Consolation

He worshipped Goethe and composed songs to his poems
He was enchanted by Heine's *Wintermärchen*
But he composed songs about a miller's beautiful wife
to poems by Müller
a lesser poet
no one would remember today
were it not for Schubert

Second-rate poets
dreaming of fame
can always count on a Schubert
who will find in their works
exactly what he was looking for

They Say It

documented

Fellini says: I am a liar
Miłosz says: I am a bad man
Iwaszkiewicz says: I know my work is ephemeral
because it can't be a basis of any faith

Once upon a time we didn't believe boasting
Now we doubt the truth of self-accusations
We know that in confessions truth is inaccessible as well

Justly

Everything costs five zlotys
Every object on this table
costs five zlotys
neither more nor less

an umbrella and a diamond tiepin
a platter and a metal buckle
a rara avis and a canary in a cage
an antique book and a laundry bill
an oar and a telephone receiver
Nikifor's paints and the comb of Violetta Villas

You can put on this table
any object you want
a notary's act and a leaflet
a violin and a pact with the devil
everything costs the same
who would want to waste time calculating the price

A Trifle

The childish pit-a-pat of Ravel's sonatina
It forgot about something and returns
it forgets something and returns
it becomes thoughtful but does not stop
it runs and runs
The enchanted little boots
don't cease to dance
until at last it throws them off
and stands barefoot

Innocence

Looking at a butterfly alight on the frame of the porch
she unexpectedly said:
At such a moment it always seems
someone is giving me a signal

When today at dawn a small bird
flew in through my window
I thought
I don't pray enough for my father

Rostropovich

Who was loved by his friends
as much as Rostropovich?
This goodness without terror
friendship without deceit or limits
He did not hesitate to give shelter
to Solzhenitsyn when he was persecuted

Who could match the impulses of his heart?
Congratulating him an English conductor   ·
almost fell off the stage backing up
before his open arms

When Shostakovich brought a stranger behind the stage
and introduced him as Mr. Benjamin Britten
he had an attack of laughter thinking it was a joke
Until then he played Britten's compositions
unaware the author was alive
Since that moment—he confessed years later—I became a faithful servant
    of Britten

I recognized Rostropovich's face and the face of his wife
the singer Galina Vishnevskaya
in the candlelight
that evening in Paris
when they were part of a crowd protesting
martial law in Poland

Today
when we want to thank him
we have only the language of music

Why Not?

The season has not yet started
The curtains of trees are still open
naked air swings among branches
the word spring has leapt onto the mellow earth once again
and begins its acrobatics

Trees already feel the high tide of sea wind and clouds
and like every year plan a great trip into the warm friendly country
for thousands of its leafy children
Everything even heavy roots seem to favor it

Why not? Why not indeed?
To try Always to try again

Wind at Night

At night the wind pushed two chairs
left on the shore into the pond
it pushed away the swan's boardwalk
moved the islet of water lilies
Since yesterday reeds at the bottom turned yellow
Time for autumn

Hades

Łazienki Park under snow.

Proserpine is asleep.

Vulcan feeds coals into the bonfire.

Somewhere Else

Calm and with a fixed stare
he didn't stop being somewhere else
because inside he was full of images
that he knew wouldn't disappear
because he wanted them and called them himself

though reason said it was all in vain
and nothing good will come from a specter

Now

Suffering but perhaps with relief and without sadness
he parts from this world where neither dignity
nor fine irony nor joking
arise
because too many of those who distinguished
between what is permanent and ephemeral
have left

If he regretted anything
it was not what is
but what was

This Is How It Will Be

It will return
There won't be any charred rubble or ruins
everything preserved as before the destruction
in full daylight and bloom

Friendship without quarreling
wells not poisoned
battles still hoping for victory

Stars not yet counted
Moon unexplored
Us still unaware
what will be fulfilled
and what taken away
forever

TRANSLATORS' NOTES

"Blues": The title is in English in the original.

"Keats's Grave": Jarosław Iwaszkiewicz (1894–1980), Polish poet, novelist, playwright, and translator, cofounded the poetry group Skamander in 1920. After World War II he was editor of the prestigious literary monthly *Twórczość* and president of the Union of Polish Writers. He received numerous literary prizes and awards.

"To Die to Sleep": The quotation in the second stanza is from the poem "Orpheus and Eurydice," by Czesław Miłosz, translated by the author, in the volume *Orfeusz i Eurydyka* (Kraków: Wydawnictwo Literackie, 2007), 21. The quotation from Dante Alighieri can be found in *Inferno*, translated by Allen Mandelbaum (New York: Bantam, 1982), 27, line 136.

"Greatness": Cyprian Norwid (1821–83), a prominent Polish poet, lived abroad most of his life. His financial situation often dire, he spent his last years in the St. Casimir House in Paris, a shelter for the poor and aged that was managed by Polish nuns. He was buried in a pauper's grave.

"The Haunted City": Jan Lechoń was the pen name of Leszek Serafinowicz (1899–1956), a Polish poet who, in 1940, emigrated to the United States. In 1956 he committed suicide by jumping from a window of his Manhattan apartment.

"The Unattainable": Krystian Zimerman (1956–), a Polish pianist, winner of top honors in international piano competitions, has performed with the world's outstanding conductors. Witold Lutosławski (1913–94) was a major composer of the twentieth century. His Concerto for Piano and Orchestra (1988) was dedicated to Zimerman.

"Justly": Nikifor (1895–1968) was a Polish folk and "naive" painter. Violetta Villas (born Czesława Cieślak in 1938) is a Polish and international popular singer.

"Why Not?": The title is in English in the original, also in line 10.